Merry Christmas
Lucy !

♡ Papa & Nana

D1016932

IN THE MANGER

25 INSPIRATIONAL
SELECTIONS *for* ADVENT

MAX LUCADO

THOMAS NELSON
Since 1798

NASHVILLE   MEXICO CITY   RIO DE JANEIRO

Published in Nashville, Tennessee, by Thomas Nelson. Thomas Nelson is a registered trademark of HarperCollins Christian Publishing, Inc.

Thomas Nelson titles may be purchased in bulk for educational, business, fund-raising, or sales promotional use. For information, please e-mail SpecialMarkets@ThomasNelson.com.

Unless otherwise noted, Scripture quotations are taken from the New King James Version®, © 1982 by Thomas Nelson, Inc. All rights reserved. Other Scripture references are from the following sources: *The Message* by Eugene H. Peterson (MSG). © 1993, 1994, 1995, 1996, 2000. Used by permission of NavPress Publishing Group. All rights reserved. New Century Version® (NCV). © 2005 by Thomas Nelson. Used by permission. All rights reserved. The Holy Bible, New International Version®, NIV® (NIV). © 1973, 1978, 1984 by Biblica, Inc.™ Used by permission of Zondervan. All rights reserved worldwide. *Holy Bible*, New Living Translation (NLT). © 1996, 2004, 2007. Used by permission of Tyndale House Publishers, Inc., Wheaton, Illinois 60189. All rights reserved.

Literary development: Koechel Peterson & Associates, Inc., Minneapolis, Minnesota.

ISBN 978-0-8499-4758-2

22 PC/LSCH 16

For with God nothing will be impossible.

LUKE 1:37

CONTENTS

Introduction   vii

1. The Author of Life   1
2. Why Would He Come?   7
3. Just Call Him "Jesus"   11
4. God Came Near   15
5. With God Nothing Is Impossible   21
6. Who Would Believe It?   25
7. Christ in You   29
8. Conceived by the Holy Spirit   35
9. Pacing Outside the Stable   41
10. Searching the Night for a Light   45
11. God Dances amid the Common   51
12. Linger Near the Manger   55
13. The Face of the Infant-God   59
14. Mary's Prayer   63
15. Joseph's Prayer   67
16. Too Busy to Notice the Impossible   71
17. How Long His Love Lasts   75

_____

CONTENTS

18. Seeing Jesus   79
19. Too Majestic for Words   83
20. What Love Does   87
21. Be Numbered Among the Searchers   91
22. Bloodstained Royalty   95
23. A Sacred Delight   101
24. Come and Behold Him   107
25. A Glimpse of His Majesty   111

Sources Index   117
About the Author   119

INTRODUCTION

A small cathedral outside Bethlehem marks the supposed birthplace of Jesus. Behind a high altar in the church is a cave, a little cavern lit by silver lamps.

You can enter the main edifice and admire the ancient church. You can also enter the quiet cave, where a star embedded in the floor recognizes the birth of the King. There is one stipulation, however. You have to stoop. The door is so low you can't go in standing up.

The same is true of the Christ. You can see the world standing tall, but to witness the Savior, you have to get on your knees.

So at the birth of Jesus . . .

while the theologians were sleeping
and the elite were dreaming
and the successful were snoring,
the meek were kneeling.

They were kneeling before the One only the meek will see. They were kneeling in front of Jesus.

The Applause of Heaven

1

THE AUTHOR
OF LIFE

Then God said, "Let there be light."
GENESIS 1:3

Seated at the great desk, the Author opens the large book. It has no words because no words exist. No words exist because no words are needed. There are no ears to hear them, no eyes to read them. The Author is alone.

And so he takes the great pen and begins to write. Like an artist gathers his colors and a woodcarver his tools, the Author assembles his words.

There are three. Three single words. Out of these three will pour a million thoughts. But on these three words, the story will suspend.

He takes his quill and spells the first. *T-i-m-e.*

Time did not exist until he wrote it. He, himself, is timeless, but his story would be encased in time. The story would have a first rising of the sun, a first shifting of the sand. A beginning . . . and an end. A final chapter. He knows it before he writes it.

Time. A footspan on eternity's trail.

Slowly, tenderly, the Author writes the second word. A name. *A-d-a-m.*

As he writes, he sees him, the first Adam. Then he sees all the others. In a thousand eras in a thousand lands, the Author sees them. Each Adam. Each child. Instantly loved. Permanently loved. To each he assigns a time and appoints a place. No accidents. No coincidences. Just design.

The Author makes a promise to these unborn: *In my image, I will make you. You will be like me. You will laugh. You will create. You will never die. And you will write.*

They must. For each life is a book, not to be read, but rather a story to be written. The Author starts each life story, but each life will write his or her own ending.

What a dangerous liberty. How much safer it would have been to finish the story for each Adam. To script every option. It would have been simpler and safer. But it would not have been love. Love is only love if chosen.

So the Author decides to give each child a pen. "Write carefully," he writes.

Lovingly, deliberately, he writes a third word, already feeling the pain. *I-m-m-a-n-u-e-l.*

The greatest mind in the universe imagined time. The truest judge granted Adam a choice. But it was love that gave Immanuel, *God with us.*

The Author would enter his own story. The Word

would become flesh. He, too, would be born. He, too, would be human. He, too, would have feet and hands, tears and flesh.

And most importantly, he, too, would have a choice. Immanuel would stand at the crossroads of life and death and make a choice.

The Author knows well the weight of the decision. He pauses as he writes the page of his own pain. He could stop. Even the Author has a choice. But how can Love not love? So he chooses life, though it means death, with hope that his children will do the same.

And so the Author of Life completes the story. He drives the spike in the flesh and rolls the stone over the grave. Knowing the choice he will make, knowing the choice all Adams will make, he pens, "The End," then closes the book and proclaims the beginning.

"Let there be light!"

A Gentle Thunder

O Lord, Author of my life, thank you for creating me in your image and starting my story. Help me write it carefully and truly become like you. Come, O come, Immanuel, and help me complete my story well. In Jesus' name, amen.

2

WHY WOULD
HE COME?

Christ himself was like God in everything. . . . But he
gave up his place with God and made himself nothing.
He was born as a man and became like a servant.

PHILIPPIANS 2:6–7 NCV

Why? Why did Jesus travel so far?

I was asking myself that question when I spotted the squirrels outside my window. A family of black-tailed squirrels had made its home amid the roots of the tree north of my office. They watch me peck the keyboard. I watch them store their nuts and climb the trunk. We're mutually amused.

But I've never considered becoming one of them. The squirrel world holds no appeal to me. Give up the Rocky Mountains, bass fishing, weddings, and laughter for a hole in the ground and dirty nuts? Count me out.

But count Jesus in. What a world he left. Our classiest mansion would be a tree trunk to him. Earth's finest cuisine would be walnuts on heaven's table. And the idea of becoming a squirrel with claws and a furry tail? It's nothing compared to God becoming a one-celled embryo and entering the womb of Mary.

But he did. The God of the universe was born into the poverty of a peasant and spent his first night in the cow's feed trough. The God of the universe left the glory of heaven and moved into our neighborhood. Who could have imagined he would do such a thing?

Why? He loves to be with the ones he loves.

Dr. Maxwell Maltz tells a remarkable story of a love like this. A man had been burned and disfigured in a fire while attempting to save his parents from a burning house, but he couldn't get to them. They perished. He mistakenly interpreted his pain as God's punishment. The man would not let anyone see him—not even his wife.

She went to Dr. Maltz, a plastic surgeon, for help. He told her not to worry. "I can restore his face."

The wife was unenthused. Her husband had repeatedly refused any help. She knew he would again.

Then why her visit? "I want you to disfigure my face so I can be like him! If I can share his pain, maybe he'll let me back in his life."

Dr. Maltz was shocked. He denied her request but was so moved by her love that he went to speak with her husband. Knocking on the man's bedroom door, he called loudly. "I'm a plastic surgeon, and I can restore your face." No response. "Please come out." Again there was no answer.

Still speaking through the door, Dr. Maltz told the man of his wife's proposal. "She wants me to disfigure her face, to make her face like yours in the hope that you let her back into your life. That's how much she loves you."

There was a brief moment of silence, and then, ever so slowly, the doorknob began to turn.

The way the woman felt for her husband is the way God feels about us. But he did more than make the offer. He took on our face, our disfigurement. He became like us. Just look at the places he was willing to go: feed troughs, carpentry shops, badlands, and cemeteries. The places he went to reach us show how far he will go to touch us.

He loves to be with the ones he loves.

Next Door Savior

Great God of the universe, I am amazed that you would leave the glory of heaven and become like me. I come to you with my disfigurement and ask you to touch me with your love. I want to be with you as well. In Jesus' name, amen.

3

Just Call Him "Jesus"

Behold, the virgin shall conceive and bear a
Son, and shall call His name Immanuel.

Isaiah 7:14

It was about to begin—God's plan for humanity, crafted in the halls of heaven and carried out on the plains of earth. Only holiness could have imagined it. Only divinity could have enacted it. Only righteousness could have endured it.

And once the plan began, there would be no turning back. The Creator knew it. The Son knew it. And soon, earth itself would witness heaven's majesty alighting on the planet.

When God chose to reveal himself to mankind, what medium did he use? A book? No, that was secondary. A church? No, that was consequential. A moral code? No. To limit God's revelation to a cold list of dos and don'ts is as tragic as looking at a Colorado road map and saying that you'd seen the Rockies.

When God chose to reveal himself, he did so through a human body. The hand that touched the leper had dirt under its nails. The feet upon which the woman wept were calloused and dusty. And his tears . . . oh, don't miss the tears . . . they came from a heart as broken as yours or mine ever has been.

So, people came to him. My, how they came to him!

They came at night; they touched him as he walked down the street; they followed him around the sea; they invited him into their homes and placed their children at his feet. Why? Because he refused to be a statue in a cathedral or a priest in an elevated pulpit. He chose instead to be Jesus.

There was not a hint of one person who was afraid to draw near him. There were those who mocked him, were envious of him, and misunderstood him. There were those who revered him. But no one considered him too holy or too divine to touch.

There was not one person who was reluctant to approach him for fear of being rejected.

Remember that the next time you find yourself amazed at your own failures.

Or the next time acidic accusations burn holes in your soul.

Or the next time you see a cold cathedral or hear a lifeless liturgy.

Remember. It is man who creates the distance. It is Jesus who builds the bridge.

God Came Near

Loving Father, thank you for sending your Son and revealing your broken heart and tears. I welcome your invitation to call your Son, Jesus, my Savior. Despite my failures, I draw near to you without fear because of your love. In Jesus' name, amen.

4

GOD CAME NEAR

For unto us a Child is born, unto us a Son is given;
and the government will be upon His shoulder. And
His name will be called Wonderful, Counselor,
Mighty God, Everlasting Father, Prince of Peace.

ISAIAH 9:6

I t all happened in a moment, a most remarkable moment.

As moments go, that one appeared no different than any other. It came and it went. It was one of the countless moments that have marked time since eternity became measurable.

But in reality, that particular moment was like none other. For through that segment of time a spectacular thing occurred. God became a man. While the creatures of earth walked unaware, Divinity arrived. Heaven opened herself and placed her most precious one in a human womb.

The omnipotent, in one instant, made himself breakable. He who had been spirit became pierceable. He who was larger than the universe became an embryo. And he who sustains the world with a word chose to be dependent upon the nourishment of a young girl.

God as a fetus. Holiness sleeping in a womb. The Creator of life being created.

God was given eyebrows, elbows, two kidneys, and a spleen. He stretched against the walls and floated in the amniotic fluid of his mother.

———

God came near.

He came, not as a flash of light or as an unapproachable conqueror, but as one whose first cries were heard by a peasant girl and a sleepy carpenter. The hands that first held him were unmanicured, calloused, and dirty.

No silk. No ivory. No hype. No party. No hoopla.

Were it not for the shepherds, there would have been no reception. And were it not for a group of stargazers, there would have been no gifts.

Angels watched as Mary changed God's diaper. Children played in the street with him. He may have had pimples and been tone-deaf. Perhaps a girl down the street had a crush on him or vice versa. One thing's for sure: he was, while completely divine, completely human.

For thirty-three years he would feel everything you and I have ever felt. He felt weak. He grew weary. He was afraid of failure. He was susceptible to wooing women. He got colds, burped, and had body odor. His feelings got hurt. And his head ached.

To think of Jesus in such a light seems almost irreverent, doesn't it? It's uncomfortable. It is much easier to keep the humanity out of the incarnation. There is something about keeping him divine that keeps him distant, packaged, predictable.

But don't do it. For heaven's sake, don't. Let him be as human as he intended to be. Let him into the mire and muck of our world. For only if we let him in can he pull us out.

It all happened in one moment . . . a most remarkable moment. The Word became flesh.

There will be another. The world will see another instantaneous transformation. You see, in becoming man, God made it possible for man to see God. When Jesus went home he left the back door open. As a result, "we will all be changed—in a flash, in the twinkling of an eye" (I Corinthians 15:51–52 NIV).

The first moment of transformation went unnoticed by the world. But you can bet your sweet September that the second won't. The next time you use the phrase "just a moment," remember that's all the time it will take to change this world.

God Came Near

Dear Lord, it's impossible for me to fathom what it meant for you to take on human flesh and live as a man. Nevertheless, I believe in you. Help me to hope for even more—that one great day soon I'll see you and be changed forever! In Jesus' name, amen.

5

WITH GOD NOTHING IS IMPOSSIBLE

Then the angel said to her, "Do not be afraid, Mary, for you have found favor with God. And behold, you will conceive in your womb and bring forth a Son, and shall call His name Jesus."

LUKE 1:30–31

Gabriel must have scratched his head at this one. He wasn't one to question his God-given missions. Sending fire and dividing seas were all in an eternity's work for this angel. When God sent, Gabriel went.

And when word got out that God was to become a man, Gabriel was enthused. He could envision the moment:

The Messiah in a blazing chariot.
The King descending on a fiery cloud.
An explosion of light from which the Messiah
would emerge.

That's what he expected. What he never expected, however, was a slip of paper with a Nazarene address. "God will become a baby," it read. "Tell the mother to name the child Jesus. And tell her not to be afraid."

Gabriel was never one to question, but this time he had to wonder.

God will become a baby? Gabriel remembered what baby Moses looked like. *That's okay for humans. But God?*

The heavens can't contain him; how could a body? Besides, have you seen what comes out of those babies? Hardly befitting for the Creator of the universe. To imagine a mother burping God on her shoulder—why, that was beyond what even an angel could imagine.

And what of this name—*Jesus*? Such a common name. There's a Jesus in every cul-de-sac. Come on, even *Gabriel* had more punch to it than *Jesus*. Call the baby *Eminence* or *Majesty* or *Heaven-sent*. Anything but *Jesus*.

So Gabriel scratched his head. But he had his orders. Take the message to Mary.

Must be a special girl, he assumed as he traveled. But one peek told him Mary was no queen. The mother-to-be of God was not regal. She was a Jewish peasant who'd barely outgrown her acne and had a crush on a guy named Joe.

And speaking of Joe—what does this fellow know? He's a carpenter. Look at him over there, sawdust in his beard and nail apron around his waist. You're telling me God is going to have dinner every night with a common laborer and call this guy "Dad"?

It was all Gabriel could do to keep from turning back.

———

"This is a peculiar idea you have, God," he must have muttered to himself.

Only heaven knows how long Gabriel fluttered unseen above Mary before he took a breath and broke the news. But he did. He told her the name, the plan, and not to be afraid. And when he announced, "With God nothing is impossible!" he said it as much for himself as for her.

For even though he couldn't answer the questions, he knew who could, and that was enough. And even though we can't answer them all, taking time to ask a few could be a good start.

When God Whispers Your Name

Gracious Father, the wonder of the good news of Jesus' coming as a baby never grows old. And it never will throughout eternity. You were the God of the impossible then and now. May your word be powerful within me, giving me strength to believe great things. In Jesus' name, amen.

6

WHO WOULD BELIEVE IT?

An angel of the Lord appeared to him in a dream,
saying, "Joseph, son of David, do not be afraid
to take to you Mary your wife, for that which
is conceived in her is of the Holy Spirit."

MATTHEW 1:20

Matthew describes Jesus' earthly father as a craftsman (Matthew 13:55). A small-town carpenter, he lives in Nazareth: a single-camel map dot on the edge of boredom. Is he the right choice? Doesn't God have better options? An eloquent priest from Jerusalem or a scholar from the Pharisees?

Why Joseph? A major part of the answer lies in his reputation: he gives it up for Jesus. "Then Joseph [Mary's] husband, being a just man, and not wanting to make her a public example, was minded to put her away secretly" (Matthew 1:19).

With the phrase "a just man," Matthew recognizes the status of Joseph. Nazareth viewed him as we might view an elder, deacon, or Bible class teacher. Joseph likely took pride in his standing, but Mary's announcement jeopardized it. *I'm pregnant.*

Now what? His fiancée is blemished, tainted . . . he is righteous, godly. On the one hand, he has the law. On the other hand, he has his love. The law says, stone her. Love says, forgive her. Joseph is caught in the middle.

Then comes the angel. Mary's growing belly gives no cause for concern, but reason to rejoice. "She carries the

Son of God in her womb," the angel announces. But who would believe it?

A bead of sweat forms beneath Joseph's beard. He faces a dilemma. Make up a lie and preserve his place in the community, or tell the truth and kiss his reputation good-bye. He makes his decision. "Joseph . . . took to him his wife, and did not know her till she had brought forth her firstborn Son" (Matthew 1:24–25).

Joseph swapped his Torah studies for a pregnant fiancée and an illegitimate son and made the big decision of discipleship. He placed God's plan ahead of his own.

3:16

Dear Lord, help me see your hand in life's bewildering twists and knots. Speak to me so I'll understand your way when I find myself trapped in a hard place. Shine your light down upon me so I can follow you. In Jesus' name, amen.

7

CHRIST IN YOU

"Let it be to me according to your word."

LUKE 1:38

W hat must it have been like for Mary to carry God in her womb?

The virgin birth is much more than a Christmas story; it is a picture of how close Christ will come to you. The first stop on his itinerary was a womb. Where will God go to touch the world? Look deep within Mary for an answer.

Better still, look deep within yourself. What he did with Mary, he offers to us! He issues a Mary-level invitation to all his children. "If you'll let me, I'll move in!"

Proliferating throughout Scripture is a preposition that leaves no doubt—the preposition *in*. Jesus lives *in* his children.

To his apostles, Christ declared, "I am *in* you" (John 14:20 NCV, emphasis mine).

Paul's prayer for the Ephesians was "that Christ may dwell *in* your hearts through faith" (Ephesians 3:17, emphasis mine).

"Christ *in* you, the hope of glory" (Colossians 1:27, emphasis mine).

And the sweetest invitation from Christ? "Here I am! I stand at the door and knock. If anyone hears my voice and opens the door, I will come *in* and eat with him, and he with me" (Revelation 3:20 NIV, emphasis mine).

Christ grew in Mary until he had to come out. Christ will grow in you until the same occurs. He will come out in your speech, in your actions, in your decisions. Every place you live will be a Bethlehem, and every day you live will be a Christmas. You, like Mary, will deliver Christ into the world.

God *in* us! Have we sounded the depth of this promise?

You are a modern-day Mary. Even more so. He was a fetus in her, but he is a force in you. He will do what you cannot do. Imagine a million dollars being deposited into your checking account. To any observer you look the same, except for the goofy smile, but are you? Not at all! With God *in* you, you have a million resources that you did not have before.

Can't stop drinking or worrying? Christ can. And he lives with*in* you.

Can't forgive the jerk, forget the past, or forsake your bad habits? Christ can! And he lives *in* you.

Paul knew this. "To this end I also labor, striving

according to His working which works *in* me mightily" (Colossians 1:29, emphasis mine).

Like Mary, you and I are indwelt by Christ. Find that hard to believe? How much more did Mary? The line beneath her picture in the high school annual did not read, "Aspires to be the mother of God." No. No one was more surprised by this miracle than she was.

And no one was more passive than she was. God did everything. Mary didn't volunteer to help. What did she have to offer? Advice? "From my perspective, a heavenly choir would add a nice touch." Yeah, right. She offered no assistance.

And she offered no resistance. She could have said, "Who am I to have God in my womb? I'm not enough." Or, "I've got other plans. I don't have time for God in my life."

Instead, Mary said, "Behold the maidservant of the Lord! Let it be to me according to your word" (Luke 1:38). If she is our measure, God seems less interested in talent and more interested in trust.

Unlike her, we tend to assist God, assuming our part is as important as his. Or we resist, thinking we are too bad or too busy. Yet when we assist or resist, we miss God's great grace. We miss out on the reason we were placed on earth—to be so pregnant with heaven's child that he lives through us. To be so full of him that we could say with Paul, "It is no longer I who live, but Christ lives in me" (Galatians 2:20).

Next Door Savior

O Lord, live in me. May your love beat in and through my heart. May you speak through my voice. Jesus, be the strength of my soul and the fire that purges wrongs from my desires. Fill me with your great abounding grace. In Jesus' name, amen.

8

CONCEIVED
BY THE HOLY
SPIRIT

Now the birth of Jesus Christ was as follows: After His mother Mary was betrothed to Joseph, before they came together, she was found with child of the Holy Spirit.

MATTHEW 1:18

Joseph was perched firmly on his branch in the tree. It was thick, reliable, and perfect for sitting. It was so strong that he didn't tremble when the storms came or the winds blew. No, this branch was predictable and solid and Joseph had no intention of leaving it.

That is, until he was told to go out on a limb.

As he sat securely on his branch, he looked up at the limb God wanted him to climb. He'd never seen one so thin! "There's no place to sit!" he said to himself. "There's no protection from the weather. And how could you sleep dangling from that quivering twig?"

Common sense told him not to go out on the limb. "Conceived by the Holy Spirit? Come on!"

Self-defense told him not to do it. "Who will believe me? What will our families think?"

Convenience told him not to do it. "Just when I was hoping to settle down and raise a family."

Pride told him not to do it. "If she expects me to buy a tale like that . . ."

But God told him to do it. And that's what bothered him.

It bothered him because he was happy where he was.

———

Life next to the tree trunk was good. His branch was big enough to allow him to sit in comfort. He was near scores of other branch-sitters and had made some valid contributions to the tree community. Surely God wouldn't want him to leave. He had roots here.

I have a feeling you can relate to Joseph. You've been there. You know the imbalance of having one foot in your will and one foot in his. Maybe you're in the midst of a decision. It's disrupting, isn't it? You've grown accustomed to your branch. And, like Joseph, you've been a pretty good branch-sitter. And then you hear the call. "I need you to go out on the limb and . . . take a moral stand . . . forgive . . . sacrifice."

Regardless of the nature of the call, the consequences are the same: civil war. Though your heart may say yes, your feet say no. Excuses blow as numerously as golden leaves in an autumn wind. "That's not my talent." "It's time for someone else to take charge." "Not now. I'll get to it tomorrow."

But eventually you're left staring at a bare tree and a hard choice: His will or yours?

Joseph chose God's. After all, it was really the only

option. Joseph knew that the only thing worse than a venture into the unknown was the thought of denying his Master. So, resolute, he grasped the smaller limb. With tight lips and a determined glint in his eye, he placed one hand in front of the other until he dangled in the air with only his faith in God as a safety net.

As things turned out, Joseph's fears were justified. Life wasn't as comfortable as it had been. The Messiah was to be born to Mary and raised in his home. He had to push away the sheep so his wife would have a place to give birth. He became a fugitive from the law. He spent two years trying to understand Egyptian.

Have you been called to go out on a limb for God? You can bet it won't be easy. Limb-climbing has never been easy. Ask Joseph. Or, better yet, ask Jesus.

He knows better than anyone the cost of hanging on a tree.

God Came Near

Heavenly Father, I see in Joseph's life the importance of responding to your call. Help me to be like him and to have the courage to go out on the limb you are calling me to. Strengthen my faith to believe you will always be there to support me. In Jesus' name, amen.

9

PACING OUTSIDE THE STABLE

*Joseph also went up from Galilee, out of the city of
Nazareth, into Judea, to the city of David, which is called
Bethlehem, because he was of the house and lineage of
David, to be registered with Mary, his betrothed wife,
who was with child. So it was, that while they were
there, the days were completed for her to be delivered.*

LUKE 2:4–6

The white space between Bible verses is fertile soil for questions. One can hardly read Scripture without whispering, "I wonder . . ."

The innkeeper too busy to welcome God—did he ever learn who he turned away? The shepherds—did they ever hum the song the angels sang? The wise men who followed the star—what was it like to worship a toddler?

And Joseph—did he ever look up from his prayers and see Jesus listening? Whatever happened to him?

His role in Act I is so crucial that we expect to see the rest of the drama—but with the exception of a short scene with twelve-year-old Jesus in Jerusalem, he never reappears. And we are left with our questions.

My first question would be about the night in the stable. Moonlit pastures. Stars twinkle above. Bethlehem sparkles in the distance. I picture Joseph there, pacing outside the stable.

He'd done all he could do to prepare as comfortable a place for Mary as he could in a barn, and then he stepped out. She'd asked to be alone, and Joseph has never felt more so.

In that eternity between his wife's dismissal and

Jesus' arrival, what was he thinking? I wonder if he said . . .

This isn't the way I planned it, God. Not at all. My child being born in a cave with sheep and donkeys? My wife giving birth with only the stars to hear her pain?

This isn't what I imagined. No, I imagined family, grandmothers, and neighbors clustered outside the door and friends standing at my side. I imagined the house erupting with the first cry of the infant. Slaps on the back. Loud laughter. Jubilation.

But now look. Here we are in a . . . sheep pasture. Who will celebrate with us?

Did I miss something, God?

When you sent the angel and spoke of the son being born, I envisioned Jerusalem, the temple, the priest, and the people gathered to watch. A pageant perhaps. A parade. A banquet at least. I mean, this is the Messiah?

This is not the way I wanted it to be for my son.

Oh my, I did it again, didn't I, Father? I don't

———

43

mean to do that; it's just that I forget. He's not my son . . . he's yours.

The child is yours. The plan is yours. The idea is yours. And forgive me for asking but . . . is this how God enters the world? The coming of the angel, I accepted. The questions people asked about the pregnancy, I can tolerate. The trip to Bethlehem, fine. But why a birth in a stable, God?

Any minute now Mary will give birth. Not to a child, but to the Messiah. Not to an infant, but to God. That's what the angel said. That's what Mary believes. And God, my God, that's what I want to believe. But surely you can understand, it's not easy.

He Still Moves Stones

Gracious Father, your ways are so far above our ways that our wildest imaginations can't begin to conceive your plans. I celebrate the wonder of the birth of your Son, and I bow my heart to what you want to do in and through my life. In Jesus' name, amen.

10

SEARCHING THE NIGHT FOR A LIGHT

So all this was done that it might be fulfilled which was spoken by the Lord through the prophet, saying: "Behold, the virgin shall be with child, and bear a Son, and they shall call His name Immanuel," which is translated, "God with us."

MATTHEW 1:22–23

On the night when Jesus was born, I wonder if Joseph ever prayed, "Father, this all seems so . . . bizarre. The angel you sent? Any chance you could send another? If not an angel, maybe a person? Some company would be nice. Even a shepherd would do."

Perhaps he did. Perhaps he didn't. But you probably have.

You've stood where Joseph stood. Caught between what God says and what makes sense. You've done what he told you to do only to wonder if it was him speaking in the first place. You've stared into a sky blackened with doubt. And you've asked what Joseph asked.

You've asked if you're still on the right road. You've asked if you were supposed to turn left when you turned right. And you've asked if there is a plan behind this scheme. Things haven't turned out as you thought they would.

Each of us knows what it's like to search the night for a light. Not outside a stable, but perhaps outside an emergency room or on the manicured grass of a cemetery. We've asked our questions. We've questioned

God's plan. And we've wondered why God does what he does.

The Bethlehem sky was not the first to hear the pleadings of a confused pilgrim.

If you are asking what Joseph asked, let me urge you to do what Joseph did. Obey. That's what he did. He obeyed when the angel called, when Mary explained, and when God sent.

He was obedient when the sky was bright . . . and when it was dark.

He didn't let his confusion disrupt his obedience. He didn't know everything. But he did what he knew. He shut down his business, packed up his family, and went to another country. Why? Because that's what God said to do.

What about you? Just like Joseph, you can't see the whole picture. Just like Joseph, your task is to see that Jesus is brought into your part of the world. And just like Joseph, you have a choice: to obey or disobey. Because Joseph obeyed, God used him to change the world.

Can he do the same with you?

God still looks for Josephs today. Men and women

who believe that God is not through with this world. Common people who serve an uncommon God.

Will you be that kind of person? Will you serve . . . even when you don't understand?

No, the Bethlehem sky was not the last to hear the pleadings of an honest heart. And perhaps God didn't answer every question for Joseph. But he answered the most important one. "Are you still with me, God?" And through the first cries of the God-child the answer came.

"Yes, Joseph. I'm with you."

Through the small face of the stable-born baby, he says yes.

Yes, your sins are forgiven.

Yes, your name is written in heaven.

Yes, death has been defeated.

And yes, God has entered your world.

Immanuel. God is with us.

He Still Moves Stones

Father, I've faced some dark nights of confusion, and I know there'll be more. Thank you that Jesus was born and you found a way to reach me in my lostness. Help me to always see you and obey you, especially when it's darkest. In Jesus' name, amen.

11

GOD DANCES AMID THE COMMON

Now there were in the same country shepherds living out in the fields, keeping watch over their flock by night. And behold, an angel of the Lord stood before them, and the glory of the Lord shone around them, and they were greatly afraid.

LUKE 2:8–9

There is one word that describes the night he came—ordinary.

The sky was ordinary. An occasional gust stirred the leaves and chilled the air. The stars were diamonds sparkling on black velvet. Fleets of clouds floated in front of the moon.

It was a beautiful night—a night worth peeking out your bedroom window to admire—but not really an unusual one. Nothing to keep a person awake. An ordinary night with an ordinary sky.

The sheep were ordinary. Some fat. Some scrawny. Some with barrel bellies. Some with twig legs. Common animals. No fleece made of gold. No blue-ribbon winners. They were simply sheep—lumpy, sleeping silhouettes on a hillside.

And the shepherds. Peasants they were. Probably wearing all the clothes they owned. Smelling like sheep and looking just as woolly. They were conscientious, willing to spend the night with their flocks. But you won't find their staffs in a museum or their writings in a library. No one asked their opinion on social justice or the application of the Torah. They were nameless and simple.

An ordinary night with ordinary sheep and ordinary shepherds. And were it not for a God who loves to hook an "extra" on the front of the ordinary, the night would have gone unnoticed. The sheep and shepherds would have been forgotten.

But God dances amid the common. And that night he did a waltz.

The black sky exploded with brightness. Trees that had been shadows jumped into clarity. Sheep that had been silent became a chorus of curiosity. One minute the shepherd was dead asleep; the next he was rubbing his eyes and staring into the face of an alien.

The night was ordinary no more.

The announcement went first to the shepherds. They didn't ask God if he was sure he knew what he was doing. Had the angel gone to theologians, they would have first consulted their commentaries. Had he gone to the elite, they would have looked around to see if anyone was watching. Had he gone to the successful, they would have first looked to their calendars.

So the angels went to the shepherds. Men who didn't have a reputation to protect or an ax to grind or a ladder to climb. Men who didn't know enough to tell God that angels don't sing to sheep and that messiahs aren't found sleeping in a feed trough.

The angels came in the night because that is when lights are best seen and that is when they are most needed. God comes into the common for the same reason.

His most powerful tools are the simplest.

The Applause of Heaven

O Lord, I rejoice that you are the uncommon God who comes to ordinary people like me. As the shepherds did, I simply welcome you to transform my life into the extraordinary by your grace and love. Come and dance with me. In Jesus' name, amen.

12

LINGER NEAR THE MANGER

Then the angel said to them, "Do not be afraid, for behold, I bring you good tidings of great joy which will be to all people. For there is born to you this day in the city of David a Savior, who is Christ the Lord."

LUKE 2:10–11

God tapped humanity on its collective shoulder. "Pardon me," he said, and eternity interrupted time, divinity interrupted carnality, and heaven interrupted the earth in the form of a baby. Christianity was born in one big heavenly interruption.

Just ask the Bethlehem shepherds. We know so little about these men. Their names? Their ages? How many were on duty that night? We don't know. But this much we can safely assume: they had no expectations of excitement. These are sheep they are watching. We count sheep to go to sleep!

Besides, this is the night shift. Might as well watch paint dry. Shepherds watching sheep sleep? Saying that sentence is more exciting than doing their job. Their greatest challenge was staying awake! These men expected no excitement.

Nor did they want any. Any excitement was bad excitement—wolves, mountain lions, poachers. Shepherds treasured the predictable. They coveted the calm. Their singular aim was to be able to tell their wives, "Nothing happened last night."

Just because they wanted a calm night, however, didn't mean they would get it.

"Then an angel of the Lord stood before them. The glory of the Lord was shining around them, and they became very frightened" (Luke 2:9 NCV).

Change always brings fear before it brings faith. We always assume the worst before we look for the best. God interrupts our lives with something we've never seen, and rather than praise, we panic! We interpret the presence of a problem as the absence of God and scoot!

Good thing the shepherds lingered. Otherwise they might have missed the second verse.

"Today your Savior was born in the town of David. He is Christ, the Lord" (Luke 2:11 NCV).

I hope you'll do what the shepherds did—linger near the manger.

God Came Near

My Lord and Savior, I'd like to join the shepherds and see your glory, hear your angels, and know you as you really are. Open the eyes of my heart that I may behold you in your Word. I want to linger near you and know you completely. In Jesus' name, amen.

13

THE FACE OF THE INFANT-GOD

And suddenly there was with the angel a multitude of the heavenly host praising God and saying: "Glory to God in the highest, and on earth peace, goodwill toward men!"

LUKE 2:13–14

Were someone to chance upon the sheep stable on the outskirts of Bethlehem that morning, what a peculiar scene they would behold.

The stable stinks as all stables do. The stench of urine, dung, and sheep reeks pungently in the air. The ground is hard, the hay scarce. Cobwebs cling to the ceiling and a mouse scurries across the dirt floor.

A more lowly place of birth could not exist.

Off to one side a group of shepherds sits silently on the floor; perhaps perplexed, perhaps in awe, no doubt in amazement. Their night watch had been interrupted by an explosion of light from heaven and a symphony of angels. God goes to those who have time to hear him—so on this night he went to simple shepherds.

Near the young mother sits the weary father. If anyone is dozing, he is. He can't remember the last time he sat down. And now that Mary and the baby are comfortable, he leans against the wall of the stable and feels his eyes grow heavy. The mystery of the event puzzles him. But he hasn't the energy to wrestle with the questions. What's important is that the baby is fine and that Mary is safe. As sleep comes, he remembers the name the angel told him to use . . . Jesus.

Wide awake is Mary. My, how young she looks! Her head rests on the soft leather of Joseph's saddle. The pain has been eclipsed by wonder. She looks into the face of the baby. Her son. Her Lord. His Majesty. At this point in history, the human being who best understands who God is and what he is doing is a teenage girl in a smelly stable. She can't take her eyes off him. Somehow Mary knows she is holding God. *So this is he.* She remembers the words of the angel. "Of His kingdom there will be no end" (Luke 1:33).

He looks like anything but a king. His face is prunish and red. His cry, though strong and healthy, is still the helpless and piercing cry of a baby. And he is absolutely dependent upon Mary for his well-being.

Majesty in the midst of the mundane. Holiness in the filth of sheep manure and sweat. Divinity entering the world on the floor of a stable, through the womb of a teenager, and in the presence of a carpenter.

She touches the face of the infant-God. *How long was your journey?*

The baby had overlooked the universe. These rags keeping him warm were the robes of eternity. His golden throne room had been abandoned in favor of a dirty sheep pen. And worshiping angels had been replaced with kind but bewildered shepherds.

God Came Near

Dear Lord, as amazing as it is that you would be born to Mary and be worshiped by shepherds, I am even more amazed that you would invite me to receive you into my life. I am overwhelmed by your grace and humbled by your humility. Gladly I offer my worship. In Jesus' name, amen.

14

MARY'S PRAYER

But when the fullness of the time had come, God
sent forth His Son, born of a woman, born under
the law, to redeem those who were under the law,
that we might receive the adoption as sons.

GALATIANS 4:4–5

God. O infant-God. Heaven's fairest child. Conceived by the union of divine grace with our disgrace. Sleep well. Sleep well. Bask in the coolness of this night bright with diamonds. Sleep well, for the heat of anger simmers nearby. Enjoy the silence of the crib, for the noise of confusion rumbles in your future.

Rest well, tiny hands. For though you belong to a king, you will touch no satin, own no gold. You will grasp no pen, guide no brush. No, your tiny hands are reserved for works more precious:

to touch a leper's open wound,

to wipe a widow's weary tear,

to claw the ground of Gethsemane.

Your hands, so tiny, so tender, so white—clutched tonight in an infant's fist. They aren't destined to hold a scepter or wave from a palace balcony. They are reserved instead for a Roman spike that will staple them to a Roman cross.

Sleep deeply, tiny eyes. Sleep while you can. For soon the blurriness will clear and you will see the mess we have made of your world.

You will see our nakedness, for we cannot hide.

You will see our selfishness, for we cannot give.

You will see our pain, for we cannot heal.

O eyes that will see hell's darkest pit and witness her ugly prince . . . sleep, please sleep; sleep while you can.

God Came Near

Loving Father, your Son came into our broken world to redeem us from our sin and make a way for us to be adopted into your family. Thank you, Jesus, for paying the price, for I was helpless to pay it myself. Help me to live today as your child. In Jesus' name, amen.

15

JOSEPH'S PRAYER

*Then Simeon blessed them, and said to Mary His mother,
"Behold, this Child is destined for the fall and rising of
many in Israel, and for a sign which will be spoken against
(yes, a sword will pierce through your own soul also),
that the thoughts of many hearts may be revealed."*

LUKE 2:34–35

God. O infant-God. Heaven's fairest child. Savor the sweet safety of my arms, for a day is soon coming when I cannot protect you.

Lie still, tiny mouth. Lie still, mouth from which eternity will speak.

Tiny tongue that will summon the dead,
that will define grace,
that will silence our foolishness.

Rosebud lips—upon which ride a starborn kiss of forgiveness to those who believe you, and of death to those who deny you—lie still.

And tiny feet cupped in the palm of my hand, rest. For many difficult steps lie ahead of you.

Do you taste the dust of the trails you will travel?
Do you feel the cold sea water upon which you will walk?
Do you wrench at the invasion of the nail you will bear?
Do you fear the steep descent down the spiral staircase into Satan's domain?
Rest, tiny feet. Rest today so that tomorrow you

———

might walk with power. Rest. For millions will follow in your steps.

And little heart . . . holy . . . pumping the blood of life through the universe: How many times will we break you?

You'll be torn by the thorns of our accusations.

You'll be ravaged by the cancer of our sin.

You'll be crushed under the weight of your own sorrow.

And you'll be pierced by the spear of our rejection.

Yet in that piercing, in that ultimate ripping of muscle and membrane, in that final rush of blood and water, you will find rest. Your hands will be freed, your eyes will see justice, your lips will smile, and your feet will carry you home.

And there you'll rest again—this time in the embrace of your Father.

God Came Near

O Lord, how can I ever thank you enough for giving your entire life that I might be kissed by forgiveness? You bore the thorns of my accusations and the piercing of my rejection. I rejoice that today I can follow in your steps. In Jesus' name, amen.

16

Too Busy to Notice the Impossible

He was in the world, and the world was made through Him, and the world did not know Him. He came to His own, and His own did not receive Him.

John 1:10–11

The noise and the bustle began earlier than usual in the village. Vendors were positioning themselves on the corners of the most heavily traveled avenues. Store owners were unlocking the doors to their shops. Children were awakened by the excited barking of the street dogs and the complaints of donkeys pulling carts.

The owner of the inn had awakened earlier than most in the town. After all, the inn was full, all the beds taken. Every available mat or blanket had been put to use. Soon all the customers would be stirring and there would be a lot of work to do.

One's imagination is kindled thinking about the conversation of the innkeeper and his family at the breakfast table. Did anyone mention the arrival of the young couple the night before? Did anyone ask about their welfare or comment on the pregnancy of the girl on the donkey? Perhaps someone raised the subject. But, at best, it was raised, not discussed. There was nothing *that* novel about them. They were, possibly, one of several families turned away that night.

Besides, who had time to talk about them when

———

there was so much excitement in the air? Augustus did the economy of Bethlehem a favor when he decreed that a census should be taken. Who could remember when such commerce had hit the village?

No, it is doubtful that anyone mentioned the couple's arrival or wondered about the condition of the girl. They were too busy. The day was upon them. The day's bread had to be made. The morning's chores had to be done. There was too much to do to imagine that the impossible had occurred.

God had entered the world as a baby.

Meanwhile the city hummed. The merchants were unaware that God had visited their planet. The innkeeper would never believe that he had just sent God into the cold. And the people would scoff at anyone who told them the Messiah lay in the arms of a teenager on the outskirts of their village. They were all too busy to consider the possibility.

Those who missed his Majesty's arrival missed it not because of evil acts or malice; no, they missed it because they simply weren't looking.

Little has changed in the last two thousand years, has it?

God Came Near

Gracious Father, I am caught in the busyness of everyday life, and it is easy to miss what you are doing in my life today. Slow me down and open my eyes, Lord. Make your presence known that I may behold you doing the impossible. In Jesus' name, amen.

17

How Long
His Love
Lasts

*For God so loved the world that He gave His
only begotten Son, that whoever believes in Him
should not perish but have everlasting life.*

John 3:16

I f you've ever wondered if anything separates us from the love Christ has for us, God answered that question before we asked it. So we'd see his answer, he lit the sky with a star. So we'd hear it, he filled the night with a choir; and so we'd believe it, he did what no man had ever dreamed. He became flesh and dwelt among us.

He placed his hand on the shoulder of humanity and said, "You're something special."

Untethered by time, God sees us all. From the backwoods of Virginia to the business district of London, from the Vikings to the astronauts, from the cave dwellers to the kings, from the hut builders to the finger pointers to the rock stackers, he sees us. Vagabonds and ragamuffins all, he saw us before we were born.

And he loves what he sees. Flooded by emotion. Overcome by pride, the Starmaker turns to us, one by one, and says, "You are my child. I love you dearly. I'm aware that someday you'll turn from me and walk away. But I want you to know, I've already provided a way back."

And to prove it, he did something extraordinary.

Stepping from the throne, he removed his robe of

light and wrapped himself in skin: pigmented, human skin. The light of the universe entered a dark, wet womb. He whom angels worship nestled himself in the placenta of a peasant, was birthed into the cold night, and then slept on cows' hay.

Mary didn't know whether to give him milk or give him praise, but she gave him both since he was, as near as she could figure, hungry and holy.

Joseph didn't know whether to call him Junior or Father. But in the end he called him Jesus, since that is what the angel had said and since he didn't have the faintest idea what to name a God he could cradle in his arms.

Don't you think their heads tilted and their minds wondered, *God, what are you doing in the world?*

"Can anything make me stop loving you?" God asks. "Watch me speak your language, sleep in your earth, and feel your hurts. Behold the Maker of sight and sound as he sneezes, coughs, and blows his nose. You wonder if I understand how you feel? Look into the dancing eyes of the kid in Nazareth; that's God walking to school. Ponder the toddler at Mary's table; that's God spilling his milk.

"You wonder how long my love will last? Find your

---

answer on a splintered cross, on a craggy hill. That's me you see up there, your Maker, your God, nail-stabbed and bleeding. Covered with spit and sin-soaked.

"That's your sin I'm feeling. That's your death I'm dying. That's your resurrection I'm living. That's how much I love you."

In the Grip of Grace

Gracious Lord, it's beyond my comprehension
that nothing can separate me from your love . . .
or that you love what you see when you see me.
That you, my Maker and God, would die for me is
a wonder. Thank you for opening the way back to
you forever. In Jesus' name, amen.

18

SEEING JESUS

So it was, when the angels had gone away from them
into heaven, that the shepherds said to one another,
"Let us now go to Bethlehem and see this thing that has
come to pass, which the Lord has made known to us."

LUKE 2:15

God invites us to fix our eyes upon Jesus. Heaven invites you to set the lens of your heart on the Savior and make him the object of your life. But what does it mean to see Jesus?

The shepherds can tell us. For them it wasn't enough to see the angels. You'd think it would have been. Night sky shattered with light. Stillness erupting with song. Simple shepherds roused from their sleep and raised to their feet by a choir of angels: "Glory to God in the highest!" Never had these men seen such splendor.

But it wasn't enough to see the angels. The shepherds wanted to see the one who sent the angels. Since they wouldn't be satisfied until they saw him, you can trace the long line of Jesus-seekers to a person who said, "Let's go. . . . Let's *see*. . . ."

Not far behind the shepherds was a man named Simeon. Luke tells us Simeon was a good man who served in the temple during the time of Christ's birth. "And it had been revealed to him by the Holy Spirit that he would not see death before he had seen the Lord's Christ" (Luke 2:26). This prophecy was fulfilled only a few days after the shepherds saw Jesus. Somehow Simeon knew that the blanketed bundle he saw in Mary's arms was the Almighty God. And for Simeon, seeing Jesus was enough. Now he was ready to die. Some don't want to die until they've seen the world. Simeon's dream was not so timid. He didn't want to die until he had seen the Maker of the world. He had to see Jesus.

He prayed: "God, you can now release your servant; release me in peace as you promised. With *my own eyes* I've seen your salvation" (Luke 2:29–30 MSG, italics mine).

The Magi had the same desire. They wanted to see Jesus. Like the shepherds, they were not satisfied with the spectacular star they saw in the night sky. To be a witness of the blazing orb was a privilege, but for the Magi it wasn't enough to see the light over Bethlehem; they wanted to see the Light of Bethlehem. It was him they came to see.

And they succeeded! They all succeeded. More remarkable than their diligence was Jesus' willingness. Jesus wants to be seen! They were all welcomed. Search for one example of one person who desired to see the infant Jesus and was turned away. You won't find it.

I wonder if you would be willing to do the same. What matters is that you want to know Jesus. Since God "rewards those who truly want to find him" (Hebrews 11:6 NCV), he welcomes you to come today.

Just Like Jesus

O Lord, you are the Light of Bethlehem and the Light of my life. As I seek you, I want to see you and know you and fix my eyes upon you. I once was blinded by sin, but your grace has given me sight. May I behold you today in your beauty and glory. In Jesus' name, amen.

19

TOO MAJESTIC FOR WORDS

"She will bring forth a Son, and you shall call His name
JESUS, for He will save His people from their sins."

MATTHEW 1:21

Many of the names in the Bible that refer to our Lord are nothing less than palatial and august: Son of God, the Lamb of God, the Light of the World, the Resurrection and the Life, the Bright and Morning Star, Alpha and Omega.

They are phrases that stretch the boundaries of human language in an effort to capture the uncapturable, the grandeur of God. And try as they might to draw as near as they may, they always fall short. Hearing them is somewhat like hearing a Salvation Army Christmas band on the street corner playing Handel's *Messiah*. Good try, but it doesn't work. The message is too majestic for the medium.

And such it is with language. The phrase "There are no words to express . . ." is really the only one that can honestly be applied to God. No names do him justice.

But there is one name that recalls a quality of the Master that bewildered and compelled those who knew him. It reveals a side of him that, when recognized, is enough to make you fall on your face.

It is not too small, nor is it too grand. It is a name that fits like the shoe fit Cinderella's foot.

Jesus.

In the four gospels of the New Testament, it's his most common name—used almost six hundred times. And a common name it was. Jesus is the Greek form of Joshua, Jeshua, and Jehoshua—all familiar Old Testament names. When God chose the name his Son would carry, he chose a name so typical that it would appear two or three times on any given class roll. Were he here today, his name might be John or Bob or Jim.

He was touchable, approachable, reachable. And, what's more, he was ordinary. If he were here today, you probably wouldn't notice him as he walked through a shopping mall. He wouldn't turn heads by the clothes he wore or the jewelry he flashed.

"Just call me Jesus," you can almost hear him say.

He was the kind of fellow you'd invite to watch the football game at your house. He'd wrestle on the floor with your kids, doze on your couch, and cook steaks on your grill. He'd laugh at your jokes and tell a few of his own. And when you spoke, he'd listen to you as if he had all the time in eternity.

And one thing's for sure, you'd invite him back.

Those who walked with him remembered him not with a title or designation, but with a name—Jesus.

God Came Near

Dear Lord, the day is coming when at the name of Jesus every knee will bow and every tongue will confess that you are Lord. I bow my knee today and make my confession that you are my Lord. Help me to honor your great name above all else. In Jesus' name, amen.

20

WHAT LOVE DOES

*. . . that Christ may dwell in your hearts through
faith; that you, being rooted and grounded in love,
may be able to comprehend with all the saints what
is the width and length and depth and height—to
know the love of Christ which passes knowledge; that
you may be filled with all the fullness of God.*

EPHESIANS 3:17–19

Would you do what Jesus did? He swapped a spotless castle for a grimy stable. He exchanged the worship of angels for the company of killers. He nursed from a breast and was clothed in a diaper.

If you were God, would you? I wouldn't, but Christ did.

If you knew that those you loved would laugh in your face, would you still care? If you knew that the tongues you made would mock you, the mouths you made would spit at you, the hands you made would crucify you, would you still make them? Jesus did.

He humbled himself. He went from commanding angels to sleeping in the straw. From holding stars to clutching Mary's finger.

Why? Because that is what love does. It puts the beloved before itself. Your soul was more important than his blood. Your eternal life was more important than his earthly life. Your place in heaven was more important to him than his place in heaven, so he gave up his so you could have yours.

He loves you that much, and because he loves you, you are of prime importance to him.

Love goes the distance . . . and Christ traveled from limitless eternity to be confined by time in order to become one of us. He didn't have to. Any step along the way he could have called it quits.

When he saw the size of the womb, he could have stopped.

When he saw how tiny his hand would be, how soft his voice would be, how hungry his tummy would be, he could have stopped. The first time he scraped his knee or tasted burnt bagels, he could have walked out.

When he saw the dirt floor of his Nazareth house. When Joseph gave him a chore to do. When his fellow students were dozing off during the reading of the Torah, his Torah.

At any point Jesus could have said, "That's enough! I'm going home." But he didn't.

He didn't, because he is love.

Think about that for a moment. Drink deeply from that for a moment. Don't just sip or nip. It's time to gulp. It's time to let his love cover all things in your life. All secrets. All hurts. All hours of evil, minutes of worry. His love will cover all of that. Every promise broken, drug taken, penny stolen. Every cross word, cuss word, and harsh word. His love covers all things.

Let it. Discover along with the psalmist: "He . . . loads me with love and mercy" (Psalm 103:4 NCV). Picture a giant dump truck full of love. There you are behind it. God lifts the bed until the love starts to slide. Slowly at first, then down, down, down, until you are hidden, buried, covered in his love.

Do it for his sake. For the peace of your heart.

And do it for their sake. For the people in your life. Let his love fall on you so yours can fall on them.

A Love Worth Giving

O Lord, you are divine love come down, and from you we have received grace and truth. Pour your love and mercy over me and cover all things in my life—my hurts and evil and secrets. I drink in your love for my every need. In Jesus' name, amen.

21

BE NUMBERED AMONG THE SEARCHERS

*The Word became human and made his home among
us. He was full of unfailing love and faithfulness.*

JOHN 1:14 NLT

The operative word of the verse is *among*. He lived *among* us. He donned the costliest of robes: a human body. He made a throne out of a manger and a royal court out of some cows. He took a common name—Jesus—and made it holy. He took common people and made them the same. He could have lived over us or away from us. But he didn't. He lived *among* us.

He became a friend of the sinner and brother of the poor. He touched their sores and felt their tears and paid for their mistakes. He entered a tomb and came out and pledged that we'd do the same. And to all of us frightened ones, he shared the same message: "Let not your heart be troubled; you believe in God, believe also in Me. . . . I will come again and receive you to Myself; that where I am, there you may be also" (John 14:1, 3).

And how do we respond?

Some pretend he doesn't exist. They occupy themselves with what they find in their part of the world and ask no questions about the Creator.

Others hear him, but don't believe him. It's not easy to believe that God would go so far to take us home.

But then, a few decide to give it a try. They venture

out of their corners and peek up through whatever opening they can find. Each day they look toward the sky.
They, like Simeon, "wait for" and "look forward to" the
day Christ comes (2 Peter 3:12 NCV). They know there is
more to life than what they've found here, and they want
to be ready when Christ comes.

Be numbered among the searchers, won't you? Live
with an ear for the trumpet and an eye for the clouds. And
when he calls your name, be ready.

Look up, and he will reach down and take you
home . . . *when Christ comes.*

When Christ Comes

Father, I want to be among the searchers who are
always seeking Jesus. That you have prepared an
eternal home for me and want me to be with you
is the best news I've ever heard. Ready my heart
to find you. In Jesus' name, amen.

22

BLOODSTAINED ROYALTY

Mary kept all these things and pondered them in her heart.

LUKE 2:19

Y ou mean to tell me God became a baby and was born in a sheep stable?" The one posing the question sounded as though he honestly didn't know if the story he was hearing was a legend or the gospel truth.

"That he would be raised in a blue-collar home, never write any books or hold any offices, be betrayed by his own people and executed like a common thief, buried in a borrowed grave, and be called the Son of God?" He paused a second. "Doesn't that all sound rather absurd?"

The Incarnation . . . absurd? Jesus on a cross . . . absurd? At the time, the man's questions had taken my Sunday school Jesus down from the flannel board.

Then it began to dawn on me: *What God did* makes sense. It makes sense that Jesus would be our sacrifice, because a sacrifice was needed to justify man's presence before God. It makes sense that God would use the Old Law to tutor Israel on their need for grace. It makes sense that Jesus would be our High Priest. *What God did* makes sense.

However, *why God did it* is absolutely absurd. When one leaves the method and examines the motive, the carefully stacked blocks of logic tumble. That type of love isn't logical; it can't be neatly outlined in a sermon or explained in a term paper.

Think about it. For thousands of years, using his wit and charm, man had tried to be friends with God. And for thousands of years he had let God down. He'd done the very thing he promised he'd never do. It was a fiasco. Even the holiest of the heroes sometimes forgot whose side they were on. Some of the scenarios in the Bible look more like the adventures of Sinbad the Sailor than stories for vacation Bible school. Remember the characters?

Aaron, the holy priest of God, leading the Israelites in fireside aerobics in front of the golden calf. David, the man after God's heart, getting his glasses steamed as a result of a bath on a roof. Adam adorned in fig leaves and stains of forbidden fruit. Moses throwing both a staff and a temper tantrum. King Saul looking into a crystal ball for the will of God. Noah, drunk and naked in his own tent.

These are the chosen ones to carry out God's mission? It's easy to see the absurdity.

Why didn't he give up? Why didn't he let the globe spin off its axis?

Even after generations of people had spit in his face, he still loved them. After a nation of chosen ones had stripped him naked and ripped his incarnated flesh, he still died for them. And even today, after billions have chosen to prostitute themselves before the pimps of power, fame, and wealth, he still waits for them.

It *is* inexplicable. And yet, it is that very irrationality that gives the gospel its greatest defense. For only God could love like that.

The question forced me to see Jesus as I'd never seen him. At first I didn't recognize him. But it was he. The lion. The Judean Lion. He walked out from among the dense trees of theology and ritual and lay down in a brief clearing. In his paw was a wound and in his mane were stains of blood. But there was a royalty about him that silenced even the breeze in the trees.

Bloodstained royalty. A God with tears. A Creator with a heart. God become earth's mockery to save his children.

How absurd to think that such nobility would go to such poverty to share such a treasure with thankless souls.

But he did.

In fact, the only thing more absurd than the gift is our stubborn unwillingness to receive it.

God Came Near

Lion of the tribe of Judah, I doubt that eternity will be long enough for me to ever figure out why you were willing to be stained with blood that I might live. But I thank you for your inexplicable love, and I receive it in silence and reverence. In Jesus' name, amen.

23

A SACRED
DELIGHT

*For you know the grace of our Lord Jesus Christ, that
though He was rich, yet for your sakes He became poor,
that you through His poverty might become rich.*

2 CORINTHIANS 8:9

No man had more reason to be miserable than this one—yet no man was more joyful.

His first home was a palace. Servants were at his fingertips. The snap of his fingers changed the course of history. His name was known and loved. He had everything—wealth, power, respect. And then he had nothing.

Students of the event still ponder it. Historians stumble as they attempt to explain it. How could a king lose everything in one instant?

One moment he was royalty; the next he was in poverty.

His bed became, at best, a borrowed pallet—and usually the hard earth. He never owned even the most basic mode of transportation and was dependent upon handouts for his income. He was sometimes so hungry he would eat raw grain. He knew what it was like to be rained on, to be cold. He knew what it was like to have no home.

In his kingdom he had been revered; now he was ridiculed. His neighbors tried to lynch him. Some called him a lunatic. His family tried to confine him to their house.

Those who didn't ridicule him tried to use him. They

wanted favors. They wanted tricks. He was a novelty. They wanted to be seen with him—that is, until being with him was out of fashion. Then they wanted to kill him.

He was accused of a crime he had never committed. Witnesses were hired to lie. The jury was rigged. No lawyer was assigned to his defense. A judge swayed by politics handed down the death penalty.

They killed him.

He left as he came—penniless. He was buried in a borrowed grave, his funeral financed by compassionate friends. Though he once had everything, he died with nothing.

He should have been miserable and bitter. He had every right to be a pot of boiling anger. But he wasn't.

He was joyful. Joyful when he was poor. Joyful when he was abandoned and betrayed. Even joyful when he was hung on a tool of torture, his hands pierced with six-inch Roman spikes.

What type of joy is this?

I call it sacred delight.

It is sacred because it is not of the earth. What is sacred is God's. And this joy is God's.

———

It is delight because delight can satisfy and surprise.

Delight is Bethlehem shepherds dancing a jig outside a cave. Delight is Mary watching God sleep in a feed trough. Delight is white-haired Simeon praising God, who is about to be circumcised.

What is sacred delight? It is God doing what gods would be doing only in your wildest dreams—wearing diapers, riding donkeys, washing feet, dozing in storms. It's what you'd always dreamed but never expected. It's the too-good-to-be-true coming true.

Think about God's joy, which consequences cannot quench. There is a delicious gladness that comes from God that cannot be stolen. A sacred delight.

And it is within reach . . . in the person of Jesus.

The Applause of Heaven

Lord Jesus, you endured all that you did for the joy that was set before you; then you sat down at the right hand of your Father. I praise you that I can believe in you today and enter into an inexpressible and glorious joy. My delight is in you! In Jesus' name, amen.

24

COME AND
BEHOLD HIM

*What marvelous love the Father has extended to us! Just look
at it—we're called children of God! That's who we really are.*

1 JOHN 3:1 MSG

It's Christmas night. The midnight hour has chimed and I should be asleep, but I'm awake. I'm kept awake by one stunning thought. The world was different this week. It was temporarily transformed.

The magical dust of Christmas glittered on the cheeks of humanity ever so briefly, reminding us of what is worth having and what we were intended to be. We forgot our compulsion with winning, wooing, and warring. We put away our ladders and ledgers, we hung up our stopwatches and weapons. We stepped off our racetracks and roller coasters and looked outward toward the star of Bethlehem.

It's the season to be jolly because, more than at any other time, we think of him. More than in any other season, his name is on our lips.

And the result? For a few precious hours our heavenly yearnings intermesh and we become a chorus. A ragtag chorus of longshoremen, lawyers, illegal immigrants, housewives, and a thousand other peculiar persons who are banking that Bethlehem's mystery is, in reality, a reality. "Come and behold him," we sing, stirring even the sleepiest of shepherds and pointing them toward the Christ-child.

All of a sudden he's everywhere.

In the grin of the policeman as he drives the paddy wagon full of presents to the orphanage.

In the emotion of the father who is too thankful to finish the dinner table prayer.

He's in the tears of the mother as she welcomes home her son from overseas.

And he's in the solemn silence of the crowd of mall shoppers as the elementary school chorus sings "Away in a Manger."

Immanuel. He is with us. God came near.

It's Christmas night. In a few hours the cleanup will begin—lights will come down; trees will be thrown out. Size 36 will be exchanged for size 40; eggnog will go on sale for half price. Soon life will be normal again. December's generosity will become January's payments and the magic will begin to fade.

But for the moment, the magic is still in the air. Maybe that's why I'm still awake. I want to savor the spirit just a bit more. I want to pray that those who beheld him today will look for him next August. And I can't help but linger on one fanciful thought: If he can do so much with such timid prayers offered lamely in December, how much more could he do if we thought of him every day?

God Came Near

Gracious Father, I thank you that there are no limits to when you will come to us. You still come near, every day, when we come and behold you. Help me to focus the eyes of my heart on you today and take your presence with me wherever I go. In Jesus' name, amen.

25

A GLIMPSE OF HIS MAJESTY

*For we did not follow cunningly devised fables when we
made known to you the power and coming of our Lord
Jesus Christ, but were eyewitnesses of His majesty.*

2 PETER 1:16

It is amazing that we can live next to something for a lifetime, but unless we take time to focus on it, it doesn't become a part of our life. Think about it. One can live near a garden and fail to focus on the splendor of the flowers. A man can spend a lifetime with a woman and never pause to look into her soul.

And a person can be all that goodness calls him to be and still never see the Author of life.

Being honest and moral or even religious doesn't necessarily mean we will see him. No. We may see what others see in him. Or we may hear what some say he said. But until we see him for ourselves, until our own sight is given, we may think we see him, having in reality seen only a hazy form in the gray semidarkness.

Have you seen him?

Have you caught a glimpse of his Majesty? A word is placed in a receptive crevice of your heart that causes you, ever so briefly, to see his face. You hear a verse read in a tone you'd never heard, or explained in a way you'd never thought, and one more piece of the puzzle falls into place. Someone touches your painful spirit as only one sent from him could do . . . and there he is.

Jesus.

The man. The bronzed Galilean who spoke with such thunderous authority and loved with such childlike humility.

The God. The one who claimed to be older than time and greater than death.

Gone is the pomp of religion; dissipated is the fog of theology. Momentarily lifted is the opaque curtain of controversy and opinion. Erased are our own blinding errors and egotism. And there he stands.

Jesus.

Have you seen him?

Those who first did were never the same.

"My Lord and my God!" cried Thomas.

"I have seen the Lord!" exclaimed Mary Magdalene.

"We have seen his glory," declared John.

But Peter said it best. "We were eyewitnesses of his majesty."

His Majesty. The emperor of Judah. The soaring eagle of eternity. The noble admiral of the Kingdom. All the splendor of heaven revealed in a human body. For a period ever so brief, the doors of the throne room were open and God came near. His Majesty was seen. Heaven touched the earth and, as a result, earth can know heaven. In astounding tandem a human body housed divinity. Holiness and earthliness intertwined.

This is no run-of-the mill messiah. His story was extraordinary. He called himself divine, yet allowed a Roman soldier to drive a nail into his wrist. He sent men into all the world, yet equipped them with only bended knees and memories of a resurrected carpenter.

We can't regard him as simply a good teacher. His claims are too outrageous to limit him to the company of Socrates or Aristotle. Nor can we categorize him as one of many prophets sent to reveal eternal truths. His own claims eliminate that possibility.

Then who is he?

Let's find out. Let's follow his sandal prints. Let's sit on the cold, hard floor of the cave in which he was born. Let's smell the sawdust of the carpentry shop. Let's hear his sandals slap the hard trails of Galilee. Let's sigh as we touch the healed sores of the leper. Let's smile as we see his compassion with the woman at the well. Let's let our voices soar with the praises of the multitudes. Let's try to see him.

One warning. Something happens to a person who has witnessed his Majesty. He becomes addicted. One glimpse of the King and you are consumed by a desire to see more of him and say more about him. Pew-warming is no longer an option. Junk religion will no longer suffice. Sensation-seeking is needless. Once you have seen his face you will forever long to see it again.

My prayer for this book is that the Divine Surgeon has used it as a delicate surgical tool to restore sight. That blurriness will be focused and darkness dispersed. That the Christ will emerge from a wavy figure walking out of a desert image to become the touchable face of a best friend. That we will lay our faces at the pierced feet and join Thomas in proclaiming, "My Lord and my God." And, most supremely, that we will whisper the secret of the universe, "We were eyewitnesses of his majesty."

God Came Near

Heavenly Father, restore my spiritual sight to 20/20, that I might see your Son as he truly is and that I might know him for all that he is. May I proclaim him "my Lord and my God" just as truly as Thomas did. Help me to see more of him today. In Jesus' name, amen.

Sources
Index

All of the material for *In the Manger* was originally published in books authored by Max Lucado. All copyrights to the original works are held by Max Lucado.

The Applause of Heaven (Nashville: Word, 1990): introduction, chapters 11, 23.

He Still Moves Stones (Nashville: Word, 1993): chapters 9, 10.

When God Whispers Your Name (Nashville: Word, 1994): chapter 5.

A Gentle Thunder (Nashville: Word, 1995): chapter 1.

In the Grip of Grace (Nashville: Word, 1996): chapter 17.

Just Like Jesus (Nashville: Word, 1998): chapter 18.

When Christ Comes (Nashville: Word, 1999): chapter 21.

A Love Worth Giving (Nashville: W Publishing Group, 2002): chapter 20.

God Came Near (Nashville: W Publishing Group, 2003): chapters 3, 4, 8, 12, 13, 14, 15, 16, 19, 22, 24, 25.

Next Door Savior (Nashville: W Publishing Group, 2003): chapters 2, 7.

3:16 (Nashville: Thomas Nelson, 2007): chapter 6.

ABOUT THE AUTHOR

With more than 120 million products in print, MAX LUCADO is one of America's favorite writers. He serves the Oak Hills Church in San Antonio, Texas, where he lives with his wife, Denalyn, and a sweet but misbehaving mutt, Andy.